Professional Fashion Illustration

Julian Seaman

foreword by Wendy Dagworthy

ACKNOWLEDGEMENTS

The Boots Company plc

Coates Viyella

Coley Porter Bell

Wendy Dagworthy

Nigel French International Ltd

GT Hawkins Ltd

Ian Hessenberg

Lever Brothers Ltd

Lewis Moberly

Nipper

Rediscovered Originals

Rimmel

Simplicity Style Patterns Ltd

Warehouse

Fiona Westwater

Lee Widdows

First published 1995

© Julian Seaman 1995

Printed in Singapore

Published by
B.T. Batsford Ltd
4 Fitzhardinge Street
London W1H 0AH

A catalogue record for this book is available from the British Library

ISBN 0 7134 7472 6

Contents

Contributing Designers

Sarah Awaleh ● Alex Babsky ●
Antonio Berardi ● Helène Bizouerne ●
Deborah Brett ● William Broome ●
Hussein Chalayan ● Wendy Dagworthy
● Giles Deacon ● Suzanne Deeken ●
Camilla Dixon ● Pamela Doherty ●
Denise Douglas ● Ann Elmkjaer ●
Damian Emery ● Esme Ertekin ●
Stuart Forrester ● Nigel French
International Ltd ●

Emma Goodman ● Lucilla Gringer
for Lewis Moberly and Coley Porter Bell ●
Charlotte Harrington ● Peter Huegli
● Lutz Huelle ● Faizia Khan ●
Suzanne Lee ● Michael Lewis ●
Steve McGrath for Rediscovered
Originals ● Marianna sa Nogueira ●
Anita Pallenberg ● Alexis Panayiotou
● Samantha Perry ● Rachel Pollitt ●
Christine Reichenbach ● Inacio P.
Ribeiro ● Julia Scoging for Nipper ●
Julian Seaman ● Corrine Sifflet-
Seymour ● Simplicity Style Patterns ●
Stuart Stockdale ● Fintan Walshe ●
Damien Wilson ● Melanie Wilson

PUL L

stretch

Foreword

THIS book reflects the successful practice of linking student courses with work experience and projects set by the fashion industry. The illustrations include much work from students and recent graduates mixed with examples from the trade.

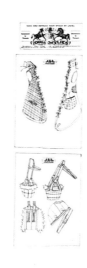 

GILES DEACON

The BA (Hons) Fashion students at Central Saint Martins enjoyed being involved with *Professional Fashion Illustration*, especially as Julian Seaman is a graduate of the college. The book shows an enormous divergence of styles and approaches to specific briefs which will encourage students to experiment in their own work.

Wendy Dagworthy

Course Director
BA (Hons) Fashion
Central Saint Martins

Introduction

FINTAN WALSHE

THERE are many diverse applications covered by the term 'Fashion Drawing'. Some perhaps come into the sphere of the fine artist, others that of the graphic designer, and there are even those which enter the area of blue print technical drawing.

IN *Fashion Drawing, the Basic Principles*, I covered the formal techniques of proportion, balance, pose and composition. This grounding will give an illustrator the confidence to break satisfactorily some rules in the diverse applications shown here.

IN *Professional Fashion Illustration* most aspects will be addressed. The fashion design merits of each illustration are irrelevant for the purpose of identifying illustrative techniques and gaining a correct understanding of the purpose the drawing is to achieve.

HISTORICALLY students have the luxury of creative and uncommercial experimentation. Despite the financial constraints of any era, this melting pot of ideas must remain.

HOWEVER, some pointers to the reality of commercial life need not stifle creative talent. This book shows what an enormous range the term 'Fashion Illustrator' can cover.

SOME of the illustrations are by fashion students who have tackled a given brief in remarkably different ways. Others are by established professionals.

THERE are many techniques used here and the message of this book is to encourage experimentation, provided that the end result fits the brief of the tutor/client.

VIEWING MAILLOT - for admiring view

SUZANNE LEE

THE garments shown in these pages may only reflect a fashion of a moment but the variety of graphic presentation techniques show that you don't have to be 'safe' to be 'commercial'.

EACH section is devoted to one specific aspect of the fashion illust- ration market, from design ideas to advertisement artwork.

HERE is a useful reminder to students that commercial constraints exist. This book was designated at 96 pages, alternating between colour and black and white spreads, before it was commissioned, written or illustrated. That was our brief.

Creativity and commercial restrictions can work together.

HUSSEIN CHALAYAN

Storyboard inspiration

In this team project the brief was to design a capsule collection for Autumn/Winter, suitable for an upmarket retail chain. The customer base is female and aged between 25 and 28.

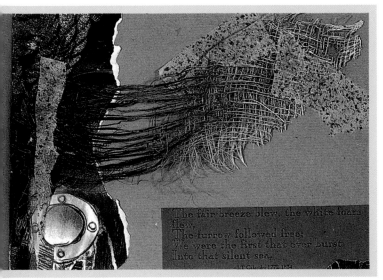

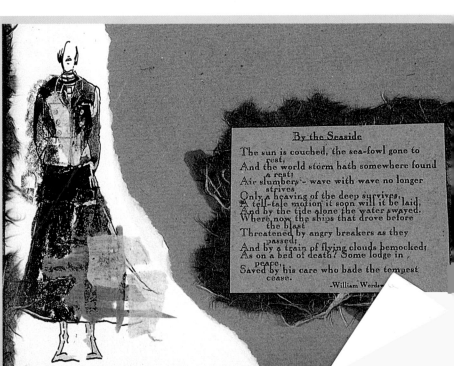

PROJECT PARTICIPANTS: SARAH AWALEH/
ALEX BABSKY/HELÈNE BIZOUERNE/
DEBORAH BRETT/WILL BROOME/
DENISE DOUGLAS/ANN ELMKJAER/
CHRISTINE REICHENBACH

f IRST the concept and mood are worked on in storyboard and sketch book form. Inspirational cuttings are included.

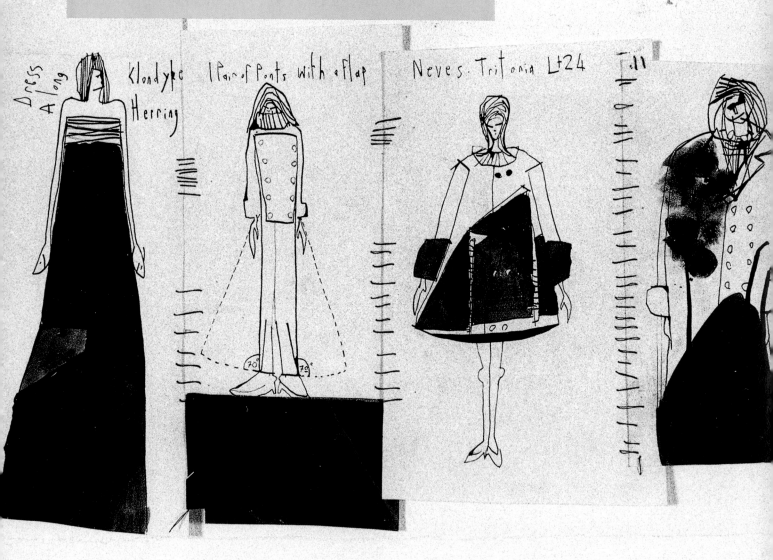

S IMPLE line drawings are matched with colour samples and swatches of textile ideas. Here a nautical theme is developed and the first draft ideas noted.

Over the wine-dark sea
-Homer c.900BC

t H E 'finished' drawings show the garment shapes, colours and whole mood of the theme. The illustrator has used gouache, ink and collage to achieve presentation images which reflect the concept of the collection perfectly.

Design
drawings

Tartan is the theme for this project. The four
illustrators have taken very different approaches.

t H E S E children's designs have been drawn as cartoon characters which are just as

effective as 'fashion' drawings with their more traditional elongated figures.

They reflect the essence of the collection well.

a | MORE sophisticated look is achieved with these pencil and gouache drawings. A well defined back view is often ignored, but is very important once a range is being considered for production.

iF the imagery is strong enough, an illustration can work just as well in monochrome. This is useful to bear in mind if drawing for newsprint publications.

DAMIAN EMERY

ALEXIS PANAYIOTOU

i N this illustration the designer has done without human figures altogether, but has created the garment shapes out of cut paper, creating an interesting image which almost falls between fashion drawing and origami.

W | I T H felt tip and collage, using minimalist figurative drawing, just the relevant part of the garment is highlighted, showing different colourways and wrapping techniques.

see how the patterns work together!

LUTZ HUELLE

t | H E variety of approach

shows the diversity of

styles used to represent

one type of fabric well.

SUZANNE DEEKEN

Working drawings

For a design concept to become a reality, detailed working drawings are essential. Earlier sketches or storyboard themes are the source and inspiration and 'finished' drawings can advertise and promote a collection. But between these two applications of fashion illustration, exact measurements and details must be recorded.

n EVERTHELESS, these drawings can still project style and image.

PETER HUEGLI

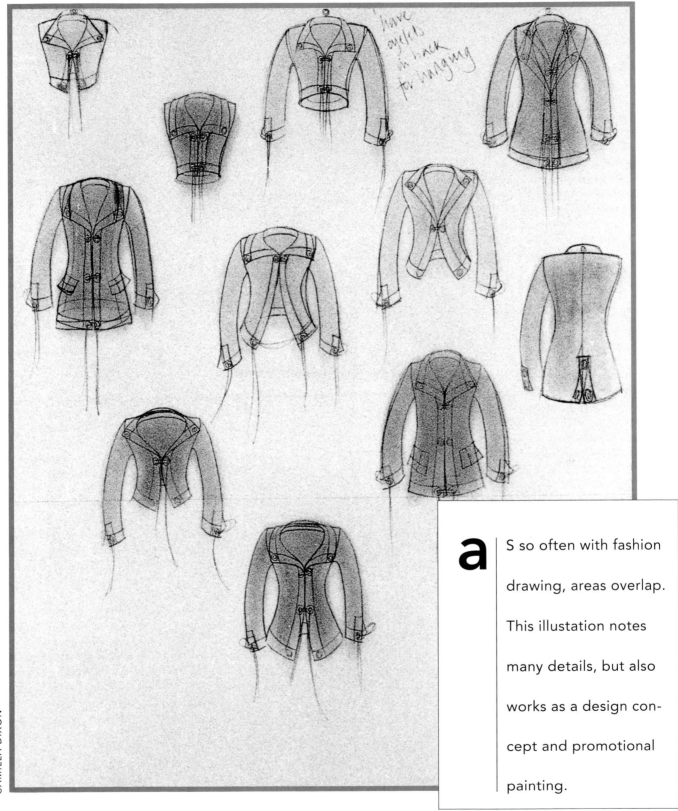

have eyelets in back for hanging

a | S so often with fashion drawing, areas overlap. This illustation notes many details, but also works as a design concept and promotional painting.

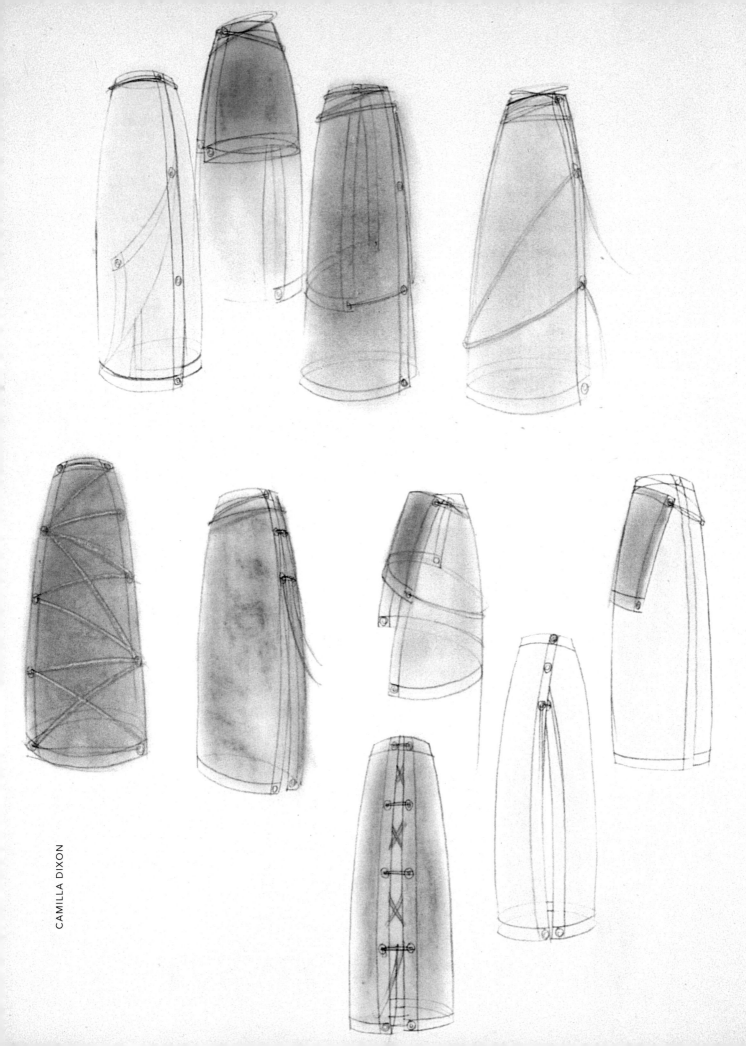

CAMILLA DIXON

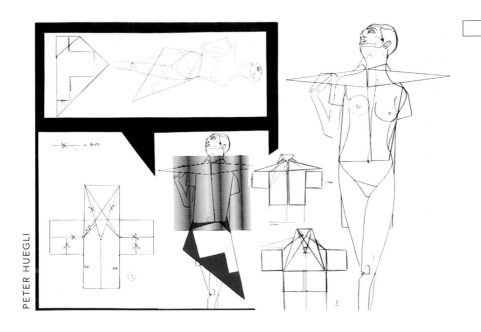

PETER HUEGLI

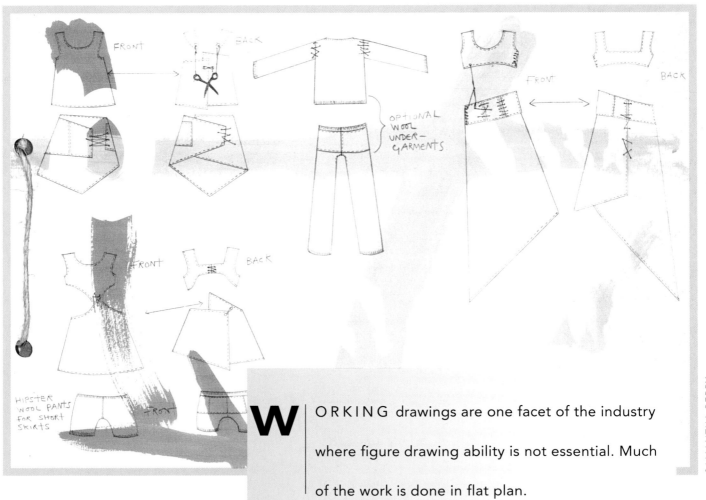

SAMANTHA PERRY

WORKING drawings are one facet of the industry where figure drawing ability is not essential. Much of the work is done in flat plan.

d ETAILS such as number of buttons, stitching and pockets must all be noted.

Catwalk sketches

A well developed sense of pictorial shorthand is necessary when illustrating fashion shows, as well as when working to a tight deadline.

j UST a few marks with some written notes can give the whole feel of a collection. The spontaneity will often produce superbly fresh sketches.

Kate Moss with breasts Westwood

Black & white

Autumn / Winter 94 /95

Black
plastic
+
purple

Hendrix
Style.

COLOUR can be

added later, since there

are obviously practical

limitations when attend-

ing shows. Time spent in

the life class will pay

great dividends, since

correct proportions will

become second

nature.

Corinne
Cobson

Autumn/Winter 94/95

Issey
Miyake

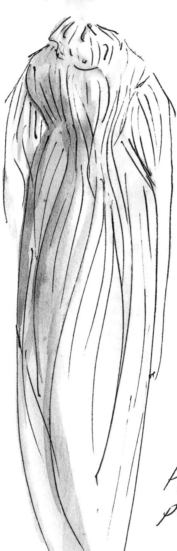

Pleats of more
pleats

Autumn/Winter 94/95

Comme
Des
Garçon

sober
army
colours

Autumn / Winter 94/95

Comme
Des
Garcon

t | H E purpose of this element of fashion drawing is to report visually the essence of a look.

extended
sleeves

Autumn/
Winter
94/95

Textile promotion

A bold statement in the design idea translates readily to the real thing. Proportion and conventional figure drawing are less important here than the colour and impact of the print. The illustration conveys the spirit of the image perfectly.

RACHEL POLLITT

b | LACK

and white

representations

can still indicate

vibrant colour.

JULIAN SEAMAN

t H E transition from concept to catwalk will inevitably involve a few changes, but it is sometimes surprising how extremely closely an original design drawing matches the finished article.

JULIAN SEAMAN

Fashion forecasts

One unique opportunity for fashion illustrators is in the forecasting business. A whole industry exists predicting the trends at least two years ahead of the market.

NIGEL FRENCH INTERNATIONAL

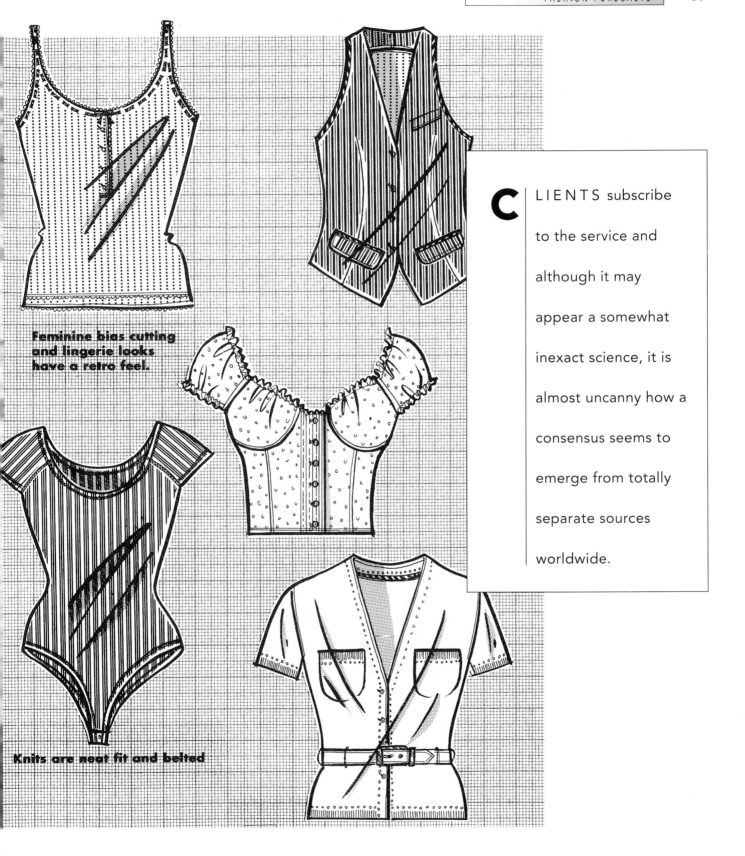

Feminine bias cutting and lingerie looks have a retro feel.

Knits are neat fit and belted

C LIENTS subscribe to the service and although it may appear a somewhat inexact science, it is almost uncanny how a consensus seems to emerge from totally separate sources worldwide.

S INCE this educated guesswork is ahead of fashion itself, there are of course no photographs of the designs – so an illustrator is the only person able to represent forthcoming looks.

memphis to vegas _____

SILHOUETTES AND PROPORTIONS

Slim fit, sharply cut – close to the body, wide shouldered jacket with flat front, narrow trousers.

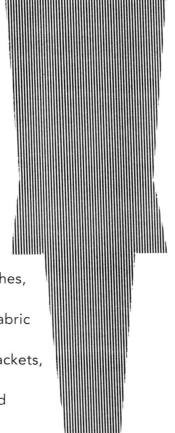

a L L aspects are covered for the client: colour sketches, print predictions, fabric tastes, lengths of jackets, widths of lapels and accessories.

new vogue

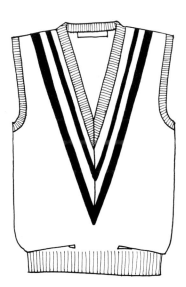

Classic cricket sweater.

Illusion layers – v-neck and short sleeves with towelling stripe inset.

Slashed neck nautical knit – wide stripes.

S INCE wholesale buyers naturally react to the information they have bought, there is no doubt that in some ways the fashion predictors have as strong an influence as the fashion dictators.

Pattern
books

Although not in the forefront of high fashion, there is an enormous market for dress pattern instructions. Drawings are used almost as much as photography in the catalogues, so this is a good area to find illustration employment.

t H E pictures must be strictly representational, but also reflect the image of the garment. Detailed working drawings are included in the chosen package.

Catalogues

With this type of artwork the illustrator is again in competition with photographers, but a well drawn catalogue can have several advantages.

i LLUSTRATIONS often depict a style rather better than a photograph can. It is also less expensive to commission artwork than to have a location shoot with models, props, stylists, photographers, refreshments and transport.

t H E watercolour and

felt tip drawings give

a perfect impression

of both the garment

shapes and textile prints

used in the collection.

i N a very different style, this catalogue uses almost photographic crayon and watercolour drawings to evoke the image.

Harry's Wool Felt Hat

— a hat for all occasions.

The point of owning a wool felt is to use it over a lifetime. As the years go by it will take on more of your personality. The problem with most hats is that they lose their strength and shape, but with a wool felt the character grows and the strength remains. *To be used and abused.* Made in the U.S.A. by the Bee Hat Company.

Colour: Earth & Black
Sizes: Sml, Med, Lge, Xlge (see hat sizes)
Ref. E51 £24.90

Uncle Jack's Trousers

We have once again resurrected Uncle Jack's cotton trousers — you just won't let them lie, will you? If you remember, my Uncle Jack used to complain, "They don't make trousers like they used to, with deep pockets, turn ups and a generous full cut, that are comfortable" (said in a Yorkshire accent). We added an extra pleat in this pair for extra comfort and slightly fuller fit which people seem to demand as much today as years ago. They also have a conventional and functional cash pocket set into the front of the trouser, reminiscent of Uncle Jack's, that has made a popular come back with fashion.

Colour: As illustrated.
Sizes: 28"-38" waist.
31" and 33" leg.
Ref. E52 £28.90.

The Co-ordinator's Document Case

During the war the co-ordinators were known as the 'back-room boys'. They were the oil that smoothed the machinery of war along, extremely important and vital to the eventual victory. They were a special type, able to cope under immense pressure whilst being efficient and decisive. Everything they used was the best available and that included this case. Our document case is made from soft full grain leather with an aged appearance. It has zipped compartments and we have added magnetic poppers on the flaps for quick release. The shoulder strap as illustrated is removable.

Colours: Rich Brown & Black
Size: 15" long x 12" high.
Ref. E53 £54.00.

16

O Scarf

.h we call this the PLO scarf, it has been adopted by many people in many
.hroughout the world, from the Palestine Liberation Organisation to the
of Mexico this is worn for protection. It protects from the sun, the cold and
.rms. And now that it has found it's way over here it is worn by men and
, in summer and winter. Ideal for biking, fishing etc.
: **Black (as illustrated) and Red.**
.143 **£4.98**

rley Key Ring

.iginal product by the original company.
.arley Key Ring is nickle silver plated on brass with
.l colouring and is an official Harley Davidson product.
F110 **£4.98**

rley Davidson
ckle and Belt

.eparately or together)

.s are the original American bikes that have successfully
the storm of Japanese competition. They have a full
.can pedigree that attracts a certain kind of person - usually
.g for freedom, with a lack of respect for regulations.
.n't offer you the bike but we can offer you the Buckle and Belt.
.ckle has been solid cast with immense detail etched into it - and later
.lled in the traditional colours.
.lt is 1$^{1}/_{2}$" wide and made from strong hide.
.rs: Dark Brown, Black
Sml, Med, Lge. (See inside back cover for details of sizes)
state colour.
F45A Buckle **£9.98**
F45B Belt **£6.00**
F45C Both **£14.98**

ck Denim Shirt

.yone who appreciates quality
.d price, a shirt for men and
that is loose fitting with
.ls and finished off with
.1 pearl buttons - not poppers.
.hat can't be beaten, ideal for
. play.
Sml. 36-38", Med. 40-42", Lge. 44-46"
F46 **£14.98**
.e shirt
t the Coming Home T-shirt at **£7.50**
F46A Both for **£22.48**

ORDER NOW
PHONE
0532 564416
FAX
0532 361790

a | CCESSORIES and
props are essential to
the message portrayed.

Accessories

Accessories are the final adornment to any look
and they can make or break the overall effect.

Hats are BIG
news this
season.

High vamped
courts or
printed keds
are key.

Work with
coloured pearls,
corsages and
floral jewellery.

i N these drawings from a fashion forecast, the background of the graph paper has been superimposed with cut outs, using rub-on texturing to highlight the tonal differences.

ESME ERTEKIN

ESME ERTEKIN

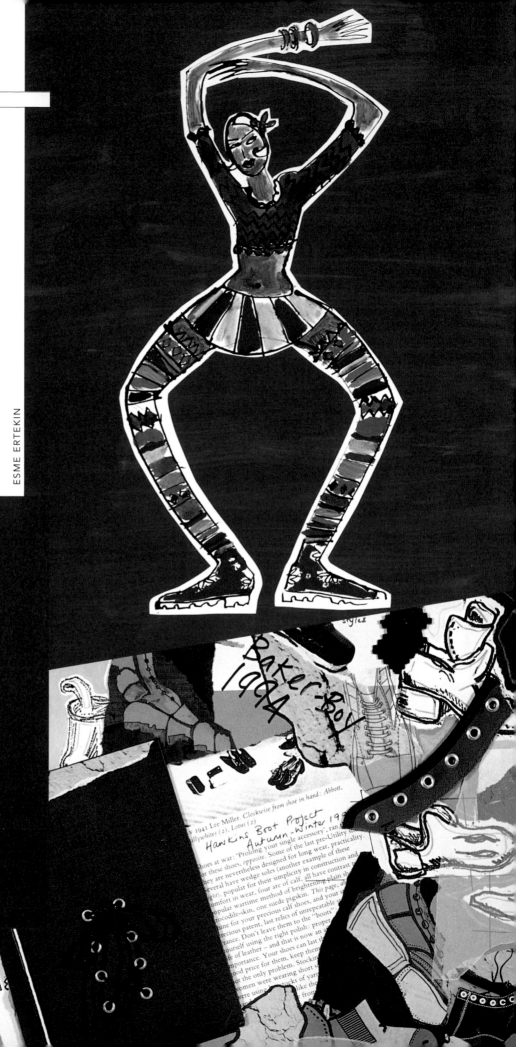

SHOES, bags, scarves, belts, earrings, bracelets, gloves, necklaces, hats, hairclips, rings, pouches and glasses are all accessories, along with ribbons, bows, ties and buckles.

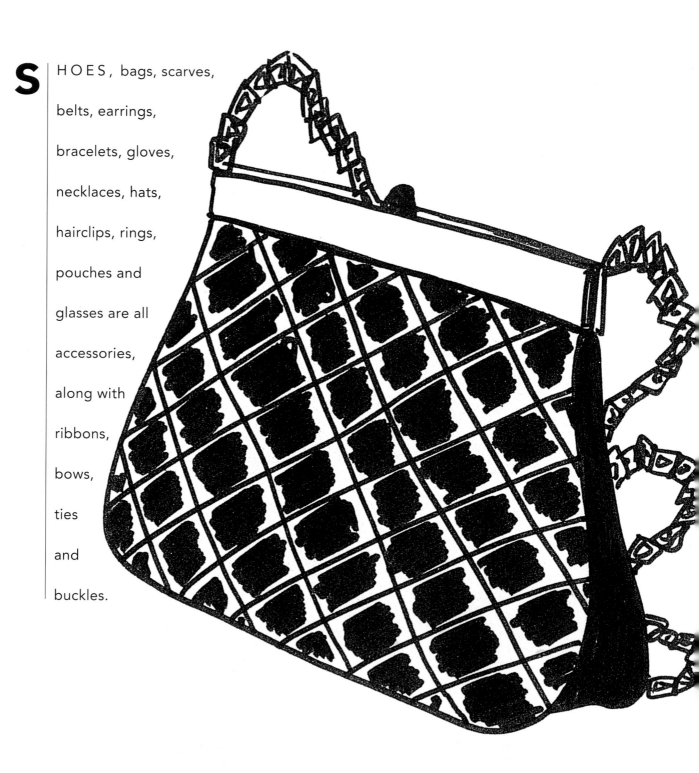

Computer pictures

Computer graphics with print-out facilities have revolutionized the scope for design innovation. Colour variations are instantly tested and three-dimensional, all round visuals can be generated.

FAIZIA KHAN

tHE technology is always improving and creativity can be at the touch of a keyboard. However, a technical facility to operate the machines is no substitute for an innate sense of design.

WENDY DAGWORTHY

Package design

Although on the fringes of fashion drawing, the packaging industry certainly produces openings for the clothes and style illustrator. Shampoo logos, hair gel containers, carrier bags and stocking boxes all have to be designed. Graphics and fashion meet in a practical commercial outlet.

LUCILLA GRINGER

SHEER TIGHTS

7
DENIER

LIGHT SUPPORT TIGHTS

SUPPORT
FACTOR 6

Boots

SHEER TIGHTS WITH LYCRA

15
DENIER

Lycra
BY DU PONT

Lycra
BY DU PONT

Make up

One way of illustrating face paint is to use the products in the drawing. Lipstick, mascara, rouge and eye shadow are perfect for depicting the items, and the colour will be correct. Tracing, montage and collage can all be used to good effect.

JULIAN SEAMAN

She's a fair creature

made up by Shakespeare   made up by Rimmel

EMMA GOODMAN

I am a woman!

MADE UP BY MOTHER NATURE.   MADE UP BY RIMMEL.

EMMA GOODMAN

t HIS work experience project was adopted by the company for their campaign. Here, a feel for copywriting, linked with design skills, created words and images which reflected the product. Cost consideration has been taken into account. These examples are just two-colour prints.

EMMA GOODMAN

tHE visual joke works just as well in monochrome.

The typeface has been carefully chosen to reflect

the pen work of the drawing.

seeds spring from seeds

and

beauty breedeth beauty

made up by Shakespeare

made up by Rimmel

JULIAN SEAMAN

'm | AKING up
| is hard to do. '

feature
illustration

Many magazine feature articles require either full page
or 'cameo' drawings. This is perhaps more a graphic
artist's role – however, since many of these pieces reflect
style, a fashion illustrator is often the best person for
the job.

X-Ray Specs

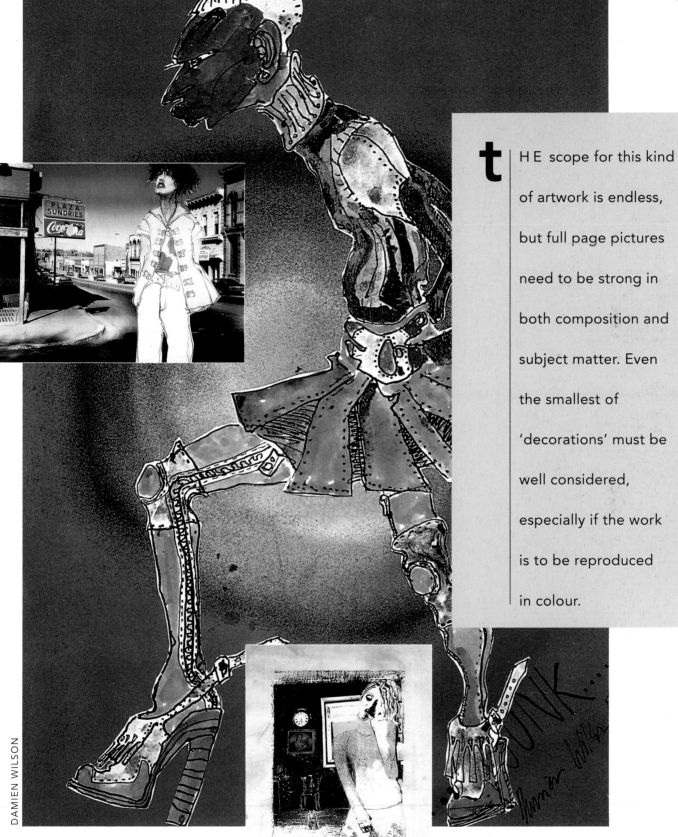

t HE scope for this kind of artwork is endless, but full page pictures need to be strong in both composition and subject matter. Even the smallest of 'decorations' must be well considered, especially if the work is to be reproduced in colour.

DAMIEN WILSON

STUART STOCKDALE

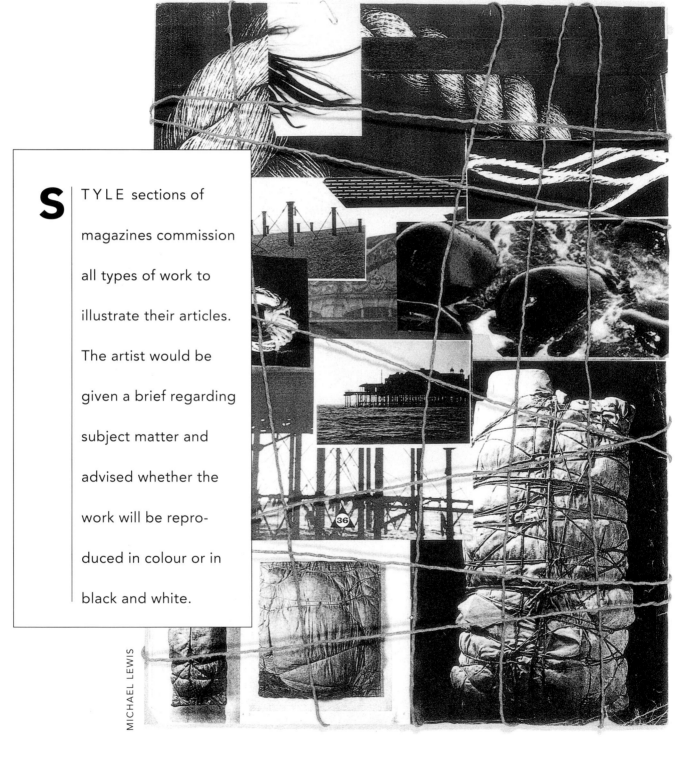

S TYLE sections of magazines commission all types of work to illustrate their articles. The artist would be given a brief regarding subject matter and advised whether the work will be reproduced in colour or in black and white.

MICHAEL LEWIS

Stage
and media

A designer's fantasy world can come true on stage.
Everything needs to be that much more accentuated.

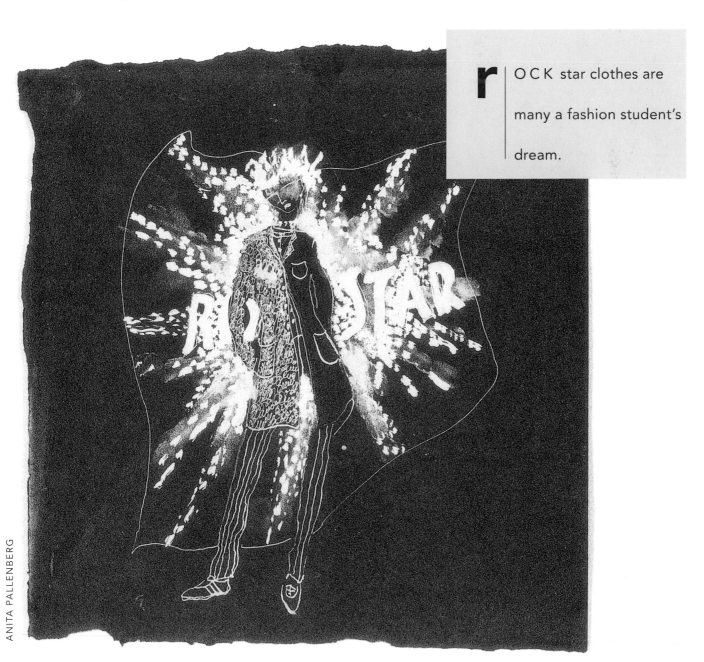

r | O C K star clothes are
many a fashion student's
dream.

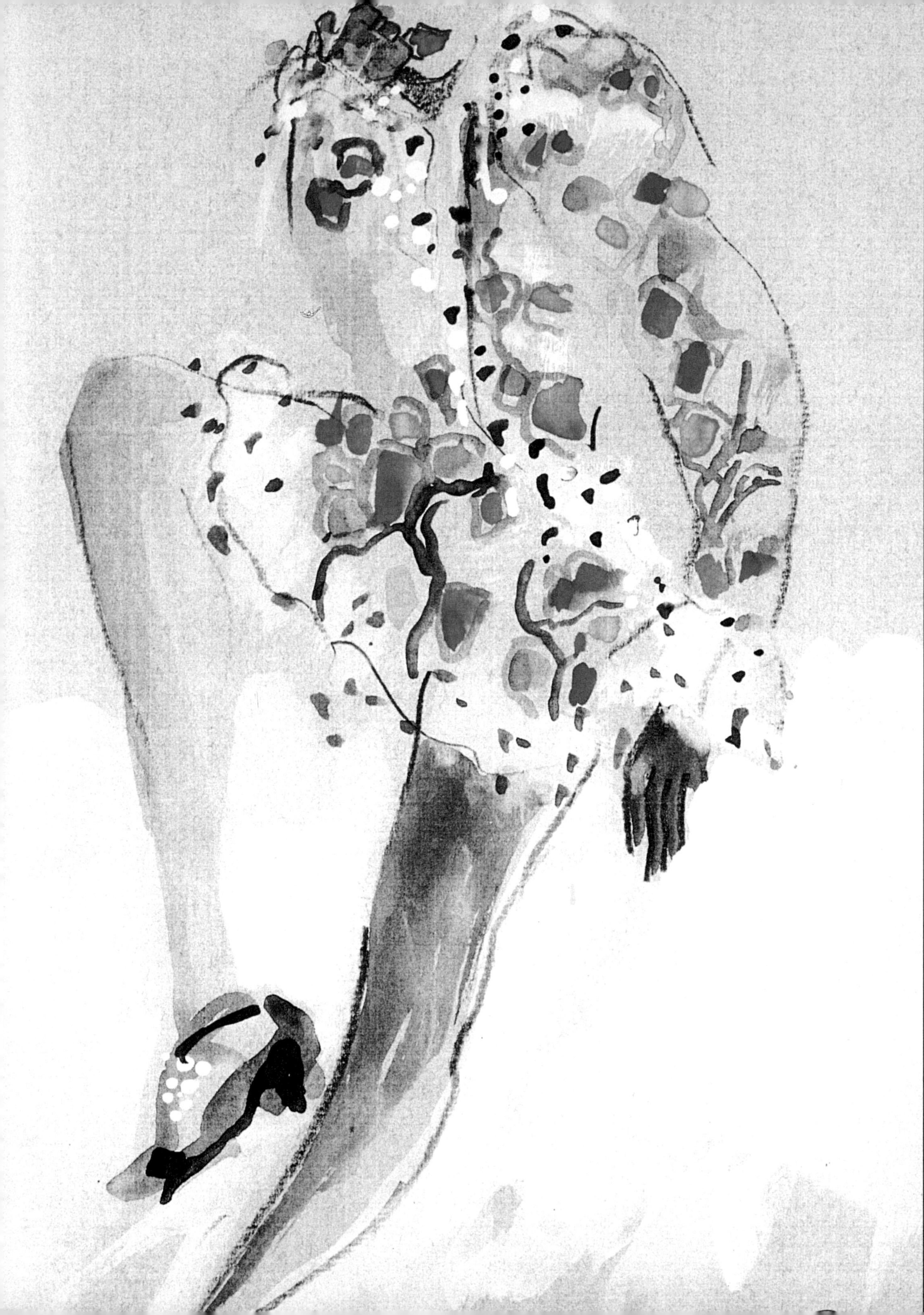

ANITA PALLENBERG

ANITA PALLENBERG

JULIAN SEAMAN

JULIAN SEAMAN

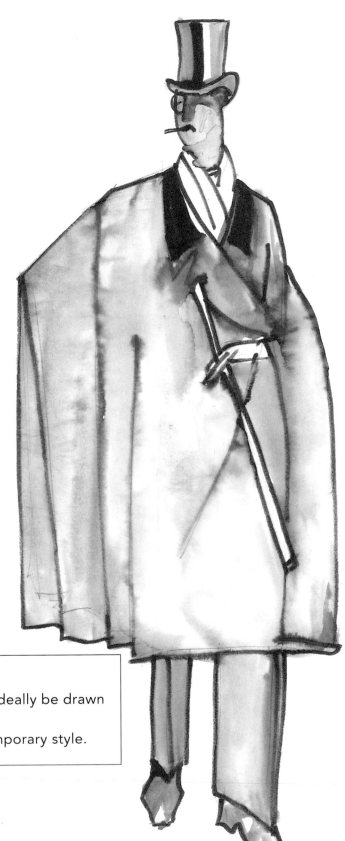

p ERIOD pieces should ideally be drawn in an appropriate contemporary style.

illustration

Finished drawings are the image window of a design collection.

PAMELA DOHERTY

CAMILLA DIXON

t H E essence of the concept should shine through, showing not just the shape, fabric and colour of the clothes, but also the statement they wish to make.

MARIANNA SA NOGUEIRA

t HESE silhouette shapes give an excellent idea of the outline of the range.

tHIS cut-out, collage, felt-tip and watercolour illustration on coloured paper is a pastiche of a drawing from another fashion artist. Ideas are there to be adapted and experimentation with styles and media can produce exciting results.

JULAIN SEAMAN (AFTER COLIN BARNES)

pROMOTIONAL copy can be illustrated with simple felt-tip sketches.

Background research

It is essential to check the potential pitfalls of client tastes and susceptibilities.

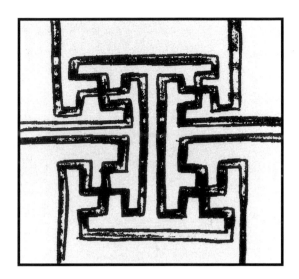

g ENUINE Greek and

Japanese designs also

include the swastika

symbol.

JULAIN SEAMAN

t | H E velvet bodice of this dress is an invented representation of a Karl Lagerfeld embroidery. The original garment unwittingly offended Muslims by quoting passages from the Koran in Arabic.

JULAIN SEAMAN

d | O U B L E triangle six point stars make an attractive design – however a print like this which shows the Star of David is unlikely to be a big seller if your client base is Arabic.

r | ELIGIOUS

sensibilities seem to

cause more fashion

problems than overtly

provocative T-shirt

slogans, like this detail

from one promoting a

fun outing. In some

countries using the

national flag as a design

is a crime.

JULAIN SEAMAN

Job
opportunities

As a fashion illustrator there are many professional openings. At the end of the day the artwork is there to *sell* – either the concept or the garment.

Your skills can lead you to be a :

○ Fashion Designer

    ○ Working Drawing Artist

        ○ Catwalk Illustrative Journalist

            ○ Forecasting Artwork Originator

                ○ Pattern Book and Catalogue Illustrator

                    ○ Journalistic Feature Illuminator

                        ○ Packaging for Fashion Allied Goods Artist

                            ○ Advertisment Artwork Designer

a | LMOST any type of medium can be used for

fashion drawing – and each professional application

has its optimum way of being expressed.

JULAIN SEAMAN (DESIGN DRAWING)

STUART FORRESTER (ARTICLE ILLUSTRATION)

NIGEL FRENCH INTERNATIONAL (FASHION FORECAST)

JULIAN SEAMAN (CATWALK SKETCH)

Portfolio presentation

When going to an interview for either permanent or freelance employment, a well-presented portfolio is essential. Over-mounting work can make the baggage too bulky, and also heavy to carry from one meeting to another. Only the best work should be included and mounts must be tidied up with an eraser or replaced when beginning to look tatty at the edges.

t H E whole fashion

business is about

presentation, so the

appearance of the work

in the portfolio is

paramount.

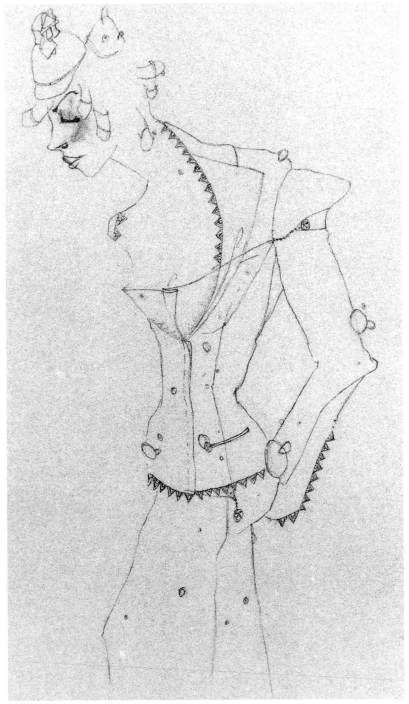

Agents

Agents can be a useful link to the professional world.

On the minus side, agents will:
- ○ take a percentage
- ○ be one step closer to your client
- ○ have other illustrators on their books who compete with you
- ○ sometimes leave you in the dark about prospects

PAMELA DOHERTY

SAMANTHA PERRY

On the plus side, agents will:
○ have the contacts
○ make the contacts
○ know the market for your type of work
○ leave you alone to be creative

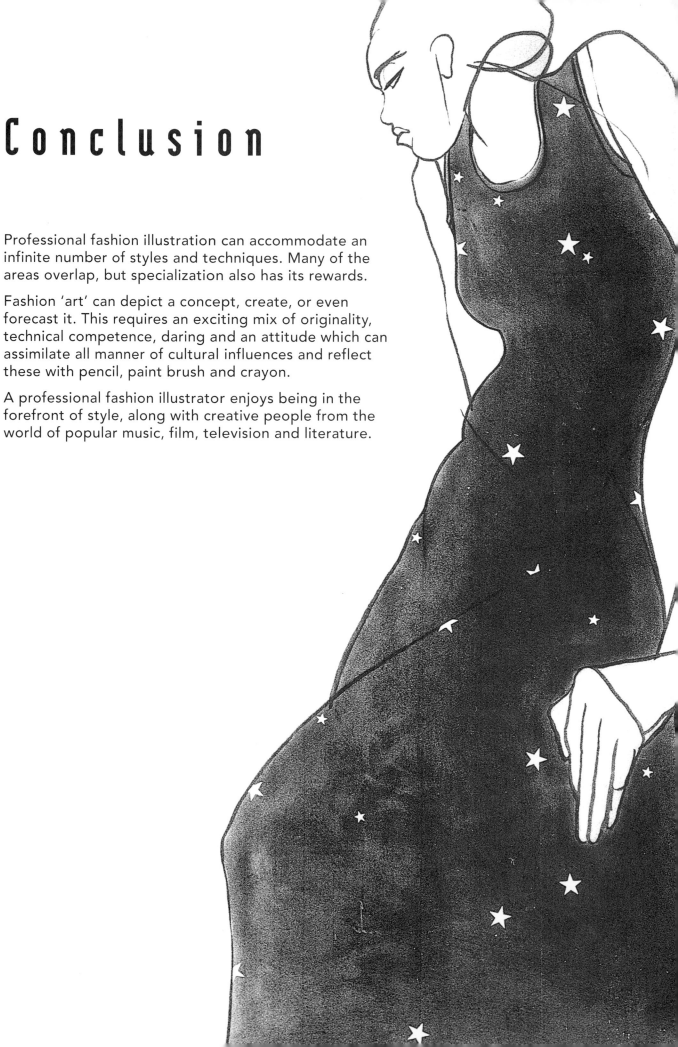

Conclusion

Professional fashion illustration can accommodate an infinite number of styles and techniques. Many of the areas overlap, but specialization also has its rewards.

Fashion 'art' can depict a concept, create, or even forecast it. This requires an exciting mix of originality, technical competence, daring and an attitude which can assimilate all manner of cultural influences and reflect these with pencil, paint brush and crayon.

A professional fashion illustrator enjoys being in the forefront of style, along with creative people from the world of popular music, film, television and literature.

CAMILLA DIXON

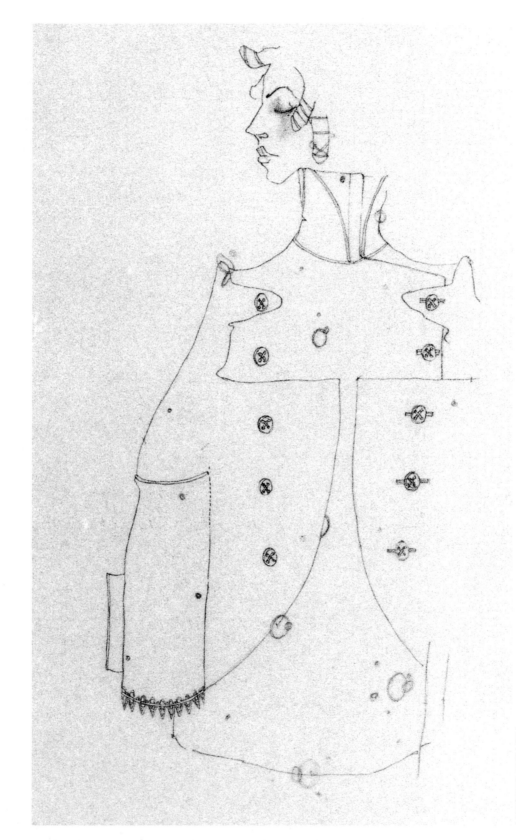

achieved a rather moving result.

The Encyclopedical Flags (fi   he
exhibition and were undoubtedly Bi
It was composed of about a dozen
embroidered with maps, diagra
complemented by substantial wr
connotation. Dozens of coun
states division, all sorts c
activities were represented

The exhibition was a f   ob
their constitution and c:
empathy. They looked like
like ingenuity common to a
overall feeling of a childh
cf the artist causing the
those objects we felt compe
his artificial world, sudden
real one.

INACIO P. RIBEIRO